How To Get High Paying Clients

Closing big ticket sales

By

Harry Perry

All rights reserved. No part of this publication may be reproduced, distributed, or transmitted in any form or by any means, including photocopying, recording, or other electronic or mechanical methods, without the prior written permission of the publisher, except in the case of brief quotations embodied in critical reviews and certain other noncommercial uses permitted by copyright law.

Copyright © Harry Perry, 2024.

Table Of Content

Chapter 1 4
Unlocking Success: Why Select High-Paying Clients? 4
Chapter 2 8
How to Draw in High-Paying Customers 8
Chapter 3 15
How to Establish Yourself as a Trusted Authority 15
Chapter 4 23
How to Find and Confirm Your Ideal Customers 23
Chapter 5 29
The First Contact in the Sales Process 29
Knowing What Clients Need and Building Trust 31
Chapter 6 49
Overcoming Obstacles in Sales 50
Chapter 7 56
How to Determine Your Product and Service's Price 56
Chapter 8 67
How to Get Things Done After Getting Paid 67

Chapter 1

Unlocking Success: Why Select High-Paying Clients?

It's critical to investigate the advantages of focusing on high-paying clientele in the quest of business greatness. These people belong to a different breed of customers than your average one.

The customers that are willing to invest a lot more are the high-paying ones; in the same amount of time, they can double, triple, or even fiftyfold your earnings. What motivates them to act in this way, though? The reason for this is that they recognize the intrinsic worth you possess.

These sophisticated people are the embodiment of what we often refer to as "ideal clients" and "long-term partners"—those you can actually make a difference and enjoy working with. Examine the following situation: To accomplish the same financial result, you may coach hundreds or even thousands of low-ticket clients as opposed to just one high-paying client. In which case, which strategy works better?

There are exactly 24 hours in a day for each of us—neither more nor less. Our goal is to increase profits while requiring the least amount of time input. Productivity is crucial; it is the ability to do more with less.

Remarkable changes in their businesses and lives are facilitated by high-paying clients who are growth-oriented and willing to use your knowledge and assistance. When you work with these people for an extended period of time, you can get a deep understanding of their needs.

Additionally, focusing on high-paying clients allows you to make more money while still having the flexibility to see the globe, spend time with loved ones, and live the life you want. By charging what you're worth, you can provide a better service and make a bigger effect without worrying about being taken advantage of. You also feel like you're being fairly compensated for your knowledge. The fulfillment that comes from knowing that the work you do is really important becomes a priceless reward.

Chapter 2

How to Draw in High-Paying Customers

How many of you have ever believed that you can't close high-paying clients or that you're too bashful to interact with the kind of wealthy clients that are necessary for selling? Such unfavorable ideas can undermine your self-assurance, breed self-doubt, and keep you from reaching your full potential.

If you are unable to discover the drive to lift your spirits, it is simple to feel defeated and afraid to take action. The well-known Star Wars proverb, "Do or do not, there is no try," highlights the significance of one's belief system.

The first step to drawing in high-paying clients is to address and change your belief system. These self-limiting ideas can impede your development, but if you adopt the correct perspective, you can open the door to acquiring valuable clients."

The Influence of Your Worldview

Your success is mostly dependent on how much confidence you have in yourself. For many, one of the biggest barriers to landing high-paying clients is a lack of self-belief. Although it takes time to change how you market and offer premium services, it is totally possible to create a long-lasting and rewarding company.

Bringing in high-paying customers takes careful preparation and reliable execution; it doesn't just happen. If you commit to creating and executing a well-planned strategy, you should witness a significant change in your clientele in a year or less.

Now let's explore the idea of believing. Over the course of a lifetime, the experiences we interpret as true or false create our fundamental beliefs. It's critical to acknowledge that a lot of our opinions are shaped by outside factors like parents, media, and social conventions. The problem, though, is that the majority of us adopt our views unconsciously, frequently as a result of incorrect readings of the past.

Consider belief as a tabletop that is unable to stand on its own without legs. The allusions or particular experiences that support your beliefs are known as the "legs" of your belief system. You can feel certain in your opinions since these references provide them a strong basis.

Take the notion, for example, that you are not a good math person. This idea is probably backed up by a ton of references, including past errors made in class, failed exams, and even remarks made by others. The 'legs' that support your belief are these references. Essentially, practically any notion you have can be validated by events.

Beliefs Influence

Now let's explore the amazing power of belief. Your convictions can be your greatest ally or greatest enemy; they have the potential to liberate you or permanently imprison you.
A fascinating story illustrates the significant influence of beliefs: Elephant caretakers have a unique technique to stop their massive beasts from fleeing: they tie a rope around a wooden peg.

On the surface, it seems impossible because an elephant of that size couldn't possibly be restrained by a rope of that kind. But insiders will just grin and explain, saying something like, "The herder uses a rope to tether a newborn elephant to a peg. By then, the rope should be able to support the elephant.

The juvenile elephant soon discovers that trying to escape the rope is pointless, and they carry this knowledge with them as they mature, learning that the rope can no longer hold them.

A moving story demonstrates the compelling force of belief: An elephant from a circus died in a fire, even though it was so strong that it could easily uproot the pole and get away. It was paralyzed by doubt because of a self-limiting belief that persuaded it otherwise.

Like these elephants, we far too frequently form beliefs that appear to have a function at first but continue to impede us long after their applicability has diminished. It's said eloquently by Anthony Robbins, "Beliefs have the power to create and to destroy."

Going back to the famous remark about belief from Star Wars that was previously cited, there is a very moving moment where Master Yoda uses the Force to raise a sinking ship out of a swamp and then effortlessly maneuvers it through the air.

Luke Skywalker says he can't believe it, to which the Jedi Master wisely replies, "And that is why you fail." This emphasizes the significant influence that ideas can have on our capacity for success and perseverance."

Changing Beliefs That Limit to Beliefs That Empower

It's important to stress once more that our own doubts and skepticism, rather than the task's viability, frequently stand in the way of our capacity to accomplish our objectives or methods. Inadvertently, these misgivings might become self-fulfilling prophecies when things don't work out the way we planned.

Our beliefs have a big impact on what we do and how successful we end up being. Thus, how can one transform beliefs that limit them into ones that empower them? Reframe your inner critic's words to something like, "If I can help someone achieve their desired results faster, easier, and more successfully than they can on their own, that's all the validation I require."

Chapter 3

How to Establish Yourself as a Trusted Authority

When individuals are faced with decisions involving purchases or financial matters, they naturally seek out experts—individuals who can provide genuine and effective solutions to their problems. No one wants to invest their time and money in someone who lacks the necessary skills and knowledge, risking disappointment and financial loss.

As a marketer, distinguishing yourself in a saturated market is imperative to attract clients. You are just one of countless professionals in a vast sea of alternatives. So, what sets you apart from the competition? What is the key to making clients choose your services or products over others? You become the recognized authority.

You cultivate a brand that is synonymous with expertise, positioning yourself as the top choice for anyone seeking the best solutions.

Declare and Accept Your Expertise.

People often have a tendency to minimize their skills by saying things like "but I'm not an expert."

While this might sometimes be true, poor confidence and self-doubt are more likely to be at work. It's interesting to note that people are reluctant to see themselves as actual experts, even after years of dedicated practice and steady achievement.

Think about it: why would a client make a sizable investment in your company if you don't believe in your own abilities?

Thus, don't be afraid to acknowledge your advantages. Be audacious and clear-cut. Take a stand and own your area of expertise. Spread the word about your abilities, and let potential clients know what makes you unique, how you become an expert, and why they should choose you over the competition.

Consider this: would a client want to work with someone who announces with confidence, "I am an online traffic expert," or someone who says, "Well, I guess I assist people in increasing their online traffic, or something like that"?

Have confidence and resolve. Accept it. Your clients will value your assurance since it gives them more faith in their choice to engage with you."

Write a Strong Introduction to Highlight Your Experience

Create a variety of approaches to showcase your experience to prospective customers. Whatever gives you the opportunity to interact with your audience and introduce yourself, use it: videos, articles, interviews, or even in-person presentations.

A well-written introduction is a powerful tool for building your reputation and persuading potential customers of your sincerity. Provide information about your services or products, mention the name of your website, emphasize your area of expertise, and include a catchy catchphrase or slogan for self-promotion.

Make sure your introduction clearly conveys your experience, lists the advantages you provide them, describes how you can help them, and explains why hiring you is the proper move."

Enhance Your Credibility by Telling Stories

It is crucial that you share anecdotes and prior experiences that attest to your competence.

Thus, using storytelling to increase your credibility is essential.

By using stories, you may establish a connection with your audience. It motivates action in addition to establishing credibility and authority.

There are separate processes that make up this procedure. Tell a story about your own hardships and journey to achievement to begin. People are able to relate to your struggles, which builds rapport.

Next, briefly outline your background and experiences while clarifying the sources of your extensive knowledge. This includes qualifications, degrees, years of experience, and first-hand trial-and-error to show why your knowledge exceeds others in the market.

Finally, tell personal success stories from both your own experience and those of happy customers and clients. Explain how their affiliation with you helped them to succeed."

Make Use of Testimonials' Power

The opinion or support of a third party has considerable weight. People are more likely to believe other people when they observe social proof, which is frequently regarded as more trustworthy and legitimate.

In case you haven't started gathering voluntary testimonies to strengthen your reputation, you might think about contacting individuals to get their opinions. Request that your contacts discuss their experiences working with you in emails.

Offering complimentary coaching sessions in return for taking part in a case study that compares before and after can be a great way to go above and beyond and get useful social proof endorsements for your blog or website.

A Successful Marketing Plan

Your credibility and positioning are greatly impacted by the way you interact and sell to your customers.

A lot of marketers still use the antiquated strategy of self-promotion, such as "Look how skilled I am; pay me, and I'll deliver."

Speaking about your skills all the time when interacting with clients can come across as overbearing and uninformed.

A professional marketing strategy would highlight how you can help customers get the outcomes they want. For example, "Do you require help? These are some approaches I can take to solve your issue. Together, let's work on this. And keep this in mind as well. For you, how did that go? Fantastic! Why don't you attempt the following action now? Please get in touch if you run into any problems."

The main type of clients looking for is problem solvers. Their willingness to pay for your services is strongly correlated with how much they trust you to deliver.

Use the appropriate way to gain their confidence. Make a good impression by providing useful and targeted solutions. Giving potential customers what they require will encourage them to say, "Please help me," indicating that they are interested.

Chapter 4

How to Find and Confirm Your Ideal Customers

It's imperative to focus your marketing and sales efforts on a certain target audience that are most likely to become customers while promoting your product or service.

Determining your target market is crucial to matching your products and services to the demands of your customers. It entails getting to know your clients on a personal level as well as their goals and financial situation.

By concentrating on a certain market, you can make sure that your company serves the proper customers and establish the groundwork for long-term viability.

Focus your efforts on establishing connections with the proper clientele who would most likely benefit from your offers, rather than trying to interact with everyone."

Segmenting the Market Effectively

In essence, a market is made up of people or organizations that are actual or prospective consumers of a good or service.

So, how do you choose the particular market niche to concentrate on? Determining the market group that has the greatest potential to benefit from your offerings is imperative. Acquire a comprehensive comprehension of the offerings your company makes to customers by identifying the attributes and advantages of your good or service.

Take anti-lock brakes on an automobile, for example. These are features that promote safety for the user.

Although features offer value to your product, people are more likely to buy it because of its benefits. Understanding what drives consumers to purchase your good or service will help you identify your target market.

This example of market segmentation illustrates how you might target a certain group of customers who have similar traits, such as families with small children."

Assessing Qualification Elements

The next crucial factor to take into account after identifying prospective target market groups is whether pursuing each of the segments that fit your business goals will be financially and practically feasible.

Here is a list of qualifying characteristics that you can take into consideration in order to help you make this selection."

Material Ability

Do they have the requisite financial means to utilize your services?

Conditions

What are the prospects' present business obstacles or areas in need of development? How important is it that the prospect deals with these issues?

Desired Outcomes

- What objectives and desired outcomes does the client hope to achieve in a specific amount of time? Are these objectives doable, and can you help the customer reach them in the time span they have set?

Expectations of the Client

- What kind of ideal clientele are you looking for, and what do you hope to achieve with these "dream" customers?"

Determination & Devotion

What degree of dedication is required from the prospect? Do they have a strong desire to accomplish their goals? Do they really want to follow your coaching advice?

Possible Diversions

What other sources of distractions would the prospect be facing that could cause them to lose concentration and attention?

Chapter 5

The First Contact in the Sales Process

Two important things that need to be addressed in the first step of the sales process are identifying the goal of the conversation and clearly stating expectations while building credibility.

Specifying the Goal of the Call

When you first get in touch with a client, you should clearly state why you are calling. Saying this is an excellent place to start:

"Hi [Name of Client], We received your application, which is why I'm contacting you. We receive a lot of applications every day, but yours caught my attention the most. I'm returning your call for that reason. Is now a good moment for us to talk, and do you remember submitting an application on our website?"

Setting Expectations and Fostering Confidence

After your client confirms that they are available for a conversation, you may move forward with laying out specific expectations and establishing your authority by saying:

"We are highly successful in working with individuals because we are dedicated to fully comprehending their individual needs. This makes it possible for us to really help.

This is how it operates: I will inquire about your past and experiences in order to tailor a "success" strategy specifically for you. We may decide together at the conclusion of our discussion whether this is a good fit for both of us. Do you find this strategy to be reasonable?

Knowing What Clients Need and Building Trust

Examining Their Predicament

In order to build mutual trust and obtain a thorough grasp of your client's position, you must successfully navigate three critical phases in the second step. It's crucial to investigate their current situation in the first stage. You can find out what they want by posing queries such as these:

"Have you had the chance to view all the videos, including those on the thank-you page?"

What particular aspect of the video convinced you to apply? What features appealed to you?

In addition, you should try to understand their history and the difficulties they are currently facing by asking:

"I really would like to know more about you. Could you describe your upbringing and life's journey?"

"How many hours are you currently dedicating to your work?"

"For how long have you been striving for success in this endeavor?"

"Is your circle of friends and family supportive of your goals?"

"What's the driving force behind your decision to pursue this opportunity now, more than ever?"

Discover Their Goals

"What is your goal? What is your long-term income goal, and how much monthly money are you hoping to earn in the next ninety days?"

(Reiterate their answer) "How do you see your life changing once you do that? What kind of effect are you expecting?"

In addition, it's critical to determine the obstacles they face by posing the following question:

"These are noble objectives... What difficulties, annoyances, and barriers are you currently facing that are keeping you from achieving them?"

"I appreciate you sharing. Do you think it would help you succeed if we could find a permanent solution to these problems?"

"Our first goal is to take the place of your present income. After that, our goal will be to replace your household's whole income. At this point, what actions do you think are necessary to replace your income? This would be our first objective."

Establishing Trust

"Building trust is an essential stage in the third phase. This process can be started by using the following language to validate and reassure your clients' decisions:

"I truly like and respect your perseverance. It is really amazing how persistent you have remained even in the face of adversity.

Furthermore, you stand out for taking the initiative to view my videos, follow the directions in their entirety, and complete the form. While many people pass up possibilities, you act on them."

"May I inquire whence you obtained this conclusion? Have you had it all along?"

Moreover, it's critical to establish a connection with your clientele by telling them about yourself and, if at all feasible, connecting, as exemplified by:

I appreciate you sharing that with me. I have total empathy for your experience. This is my personal narrative. (To establish a relationship, open up and share similar experiences)."

"Among my most successful clients, I've observed a recurring characteristic: they never gave up and continuously showed an unshakeable will to succeed. All they needed was direction from someone who had been there before and could point them in the right direction. Sincerely, I'm thrilled about your prospects for achievement."

Leading Your Customers With Knowledge

As we commence the third phase of our expedition, let us concentrate on efficiently instructing our clientele. Here, we want to actually help people by offering insightful information. Our goals are to share new insights on success, talk about typical mistakes to avoid, and outline the essential actions and the rationale behind them.

It is critical to highlight the main reasons why projects fail, such as a lack of technical expertise, a lack of mentorship and appropriate direction, and time restraints.

Let's also explore the differing ideas between the business mindset and the lottery mindset. Adopting a lottery mindset is one of the main causes of business failure.

This strategy anticipates positive results with little work. A business owner who wants to expand must have a business mindset and understand the value of capital. People who are successful in business are aware of the benefits of outsourcing, the skill of utilizing others' knowledge, and the force of scaling. They show tenacity in the face of difficulty, modifying and honing tactics until they produce the intended outcomes.

If you sense that a potential customer is inclined toward a lottery mentality, take some time in your discussion to correct and enlighten them before moving on to the following phase of the sales process. Framework for Pre-Presentation.

A crucial area to investigate is offering a formula for success. The critical components of this formula for success are talents, mentorship, good delegating techniques, and a positive mindset."

Setting Up the Stage for Pre-Presentation Framing

Now let's go on to the fourth phase, which is called Pre-Presentation Framing and involves assessing your client's overall circumstances. This procedure starts with:

Step 1: Eligibility and Commitment Assessment

- "Have you ever had the opportunity to work with a mentor or coach in the past?"
- "Are you comfortable following a detailed, step-by-step plan if one is provided?"
- "Considering your daily schedule, how many hours can you realistically allocate to your internet business?"
- "How do you feel about having someone hold you accountable?"

Procrastination is a prevalent issue. How do you usually get past it?"

Step 2: Restating Objectives

- "If we could help you achieve your income goals within 90 days, allowing you to realize your desired outcomes, is that something you'd like to pursue?"

Step 3: Evaluating the financial plan

- "Could you share what budget you have in mind for this endeavor?"

Step 4: Continuing the Video Presentation Invitation

"Are you using your computer right now? I will send you an email right away with a link to a presentation that is in video format. Please watch it, and when you're ready to talk to me, don't hesitate to do so."

How to Give a Presentation That Works

Let's now explore "Mastering the Art of Presenting Your Solutions," the fifth step. We'll discuss important topics in this area, like avoiding typical errors and choosing the appropriate presentation strategy.

Common Errors to Prevent:

Sending your proposal via email and waiting for a response is a common mistake. Although this strategy might sometimes work, it greatly reduces your chances of closing a deal. Why does it make success harder to achieve?

First of all, during the waiting period, your potential client can decide to change their mind.

They can overlook how important and urgent it is to deal with their problems.

It's possible for people to understand your suggestion differently.

Furthermore, they might not be able to see the wider picture or the possible ROI.

Usually, the best course of action is to present your proposal in person. This enables you to successfully guide your audience through it and optimize the impact.

In order to market your solutions, you must first address the difficulty of turning features into advantages. Features are the visible aspects of your product, like its specs, whereas benefits show the real results the customer will receive from it.

Consider Google Analytics, for instance. Although it has a tool that tracks statistics in great detail, the real value is in knowing how your readers behave, which can improve your web copywriting.

Consider why a feature or advantage is important to your customer if you're not sure which to choose. You've found an advantage if the response is understandable and unambiguous.

Benefits may connect with clients on an emotional level as well as solve practical issues, giving them a compelling reason to support your business. Handcrafted jewelry, for example, may appeal to buyers' demands for individuality and identification by offering the emotional reward of uniqueness.

Customizing benefits to the unique requirements of your target group is the second hurdle. It is insufficient to offer the identical set of benefits to every potential customer because they all have different goals and challenges.

You need to use insights from strategies like SPIN Selling to tie the advantages of your solutions to the particular issues that your target customers are facing.

Going on to the third issue, it is important to sell outcomes rather than just the item or service. Clients look for results that match their objectives and preferences and alter their thoughts, feelings, and behaviors. Instead of just touting the virtues of your product or service, concentrate on showing high-paying consumers how your solutions can assist them in achieving their desired outcomes in order to earn their trust.

Incorporating graphics that allow your consumers to evaluate whether they are achieving the intended outcomes will ultimately improve their comprehension and level of engagement."

Getting Ready for the Pre-Closing Stage

To help your audience go toward the closing stage as we move into the Pre-Closing stage, think about implementing the following strategies into your presentation video.

'Cost vs. Value' is the first closing method that aims to change the focus of the audience from 'how much this will cost' to 'what it's genuinely worth.'

You could ask, "What is it worth to you if you can?" as an example.

The second closing strategy that works well is to think of money as a resource. Remind them that they are investing in themselves and that they will use this money for other purposes. Why not spend money on education and personal development? Money can be recovered, but time cannot be replaced.

'Either Way You Still Pay,' the third closing strategy, highlights how investment is inevitable. They have the option of learning from their own mistakes or investing in your knowledge and experience. An investment is made in either scenario."

Finishing

"As the sales process nears its conclusion, we'll work with your client through three crucial stages.

Phase 1: 'Uncovering Values' entails talking about what follows:

Ask, "Have you had a chance to watch the video?" first. What do you think?

Secondly, inquire as to which of our packages most appealed to you, if money were no object.

Third, ask yourself, "What in particular drew your attention to that package?"

Fourth, consider this question: "Do you think your success would have been possible if you had access to what you found appealing?" Why?

Ask them if they think these will work for them, and reiterate their choices.

'Assuming the Sale & Setting Conditions', Phase 2, comprises the subsequent actions:

'Which of our packages would you like to proceed with?' should be your first question.

The second is an outline: "There are two requirements for our collaboration." First of all, would you be willing to give us a testimonial after you start seeing results from our program? Second, would you think about upgrading to one of our more sophisticated packages after you get results that meet your needs?

Thirdly, underline that "If these circumstances line up, we can proceed together."

'Envisioning the Future and Finalizing the Deal', Phase 3 includes the following conversations:

Let's be clear first: this is our procedure. After you sign up, our team starts working in one to two hours. Within seven days, you should have your operations up and running and producing results. Make quick progress if you want to achieve your goal. Are you able to keep up with this faster pace?

Secondly, make an address, We'll start creating several revenue streams for you as part of our services today. What is your preferred frequency of commission payment: weekly, biweekly, or monthly?

Third, find out which payment method is preferred: Which method of payment would you prefer—checks, direct deposits, or PayPal?

Fourth, compile the necessary contact information: "What is the main email address you use?"

5. Request the postal address: Could you please give us your mailing address?

Sixth, find out who the payee is: Whom should payments be made payable to?

Finally, say, "Great, I'm sending this information to our team immediately for quick setup," to wrap up. Which credit card would you rather use to make the payment, Visa or Mastercard?

Chapter 6

Overcoming Obstacles in Sales

While most of us may not be born with the ability to sell, it is still very much within our reach. Finding the obstacles preventing a potential client from choosing wisely is frequently crucial. Once you've identified their doubts, you may successfully answer those objections with tailored responses.

Typical Sales Obstacles

Salespeople frequently run into basic objections from their clients, such as worries about cost, the need to confer with a spouse, requests for guarantees, or the need for additional time to consider the option. These criticisms are easily divided into four categories.

Identifying the Type of Objection

You need to go deeper to understand the fundamental source of an objection's worry in order to determine which category it belongs in."

Lack of Necessity

When a prospective client meets your targeting criteria and appears to be a good fit, they don't perceive the value in what you have to offer.

Lack of Immediacy

Financial limitations are not an issue once you have built rapport, fostered trust, and made sure the client knows you can help. However, the prospect is unable to move the idea forward because of their heavy workload and waiting for the "perfect moment."

Lack of self-assurance

Whether or not a prospect believes you can fulfill your commitments determines how much trust you will earn."

Insufficient Funds

It's critical to ascertain whether this objection is legitimate or just a roadblock. A legitimate objection cannot be overcome, but an obstacle may.

Typical Mistakes

Do you respond quickly to sales objections, giving prompt responses and trying to get beyond them quickly so you can go on to the close stage? If so, it's likely that you may not be:

Asking clarifying questions to ensure that you fully understand the objection and its underlying justifications.

- Finding a comprehensive solution that gives the prospect the degree of fulfillment they want.
- Making an argument that is strong enough to go past the resistance and seal the sale.

Asia-Pacific Model

After you've put a lot of work into your presentation, there comes a moment when your prospect unexpectedly voice an issue since they aren't sold.

How did you go so quickly from being a hero to becoming ineffectual? How did you handle that objection incorrectly?

The APAC model can be useful in this situation. You should keep in mind this simple acronym for your next situation with managing objections."

Awareness

Although it may seem insignificant at first, ignoring this point completely is the worst course of action. Begin by admitting that it's a legitimate worry and start a conversation about it.

Investigating

Take some time to make sure you understand everything completely before getting started. Is there a particular reason your prospect brought up this issue? Have they previously had unpleasant experiences? Does it actually relate to what you're selling?

In response

It's time to react now that you have a clear understanding of the circumstances. Make sure you answer all of the prospect's questions; because of your extensive research, they ought to be well-informed.

Result

Finally, ensure that the problem has been adequately addressed and conclude the matter. Recall that you're one step closer to closing the deal by fixing the problem."

Chapter 7

How to Determine Your Product and Service's Price

Companies may set or modify their pricing policies at launch, when launching new goods or services, to meet new objectives, or in reaction to shifts in the market or state of the economy. Whichever the case, one of the most important business considerations is pricing your products or services. Pricing decisions have a big impact on profitability and can affect how your business does financially.

Developing a price strategy should work in tandem with your changing business plan, not independently of it. When it comes to your price targets, how they fit into your overall business objectives, and how they work with your marketing and sales strategy, clarity is key.

Different Pricing Strategy Types"

Price Plus Cost

Adding a profit margin, typically stated as a percentage of the cost, to the production cost of your good or service is known as "cost plus pricing." Typically, companies handling large numbers or competing on pricing are more suited for this approach.

It's critical to take into account and account for how price adjustments will impact variable expenses in your calculations. Furthermore, take care not to ignore unstated costs since this could result in an overestimation of possible earnings per sale.

Important components like market positioning, company reputation, and the perceived value of your service to clients may potentially be overlooked by this strategy. If you only use cost-based pricing, you may undersell and lose out on prospective sales.

Pricing Based on Value

Value-based pricing bases a price on an evaluation of the product or service's perceived value by consumers. The aim is to strike a balance between not overcharging above what clients are ready to pay and not underpricing and losing out on possible sales. The secret is to pinpoint the advantages you offer and make sure your clients are aware of and appreciate them.

You can set your prices according to the value you provide if you have unique advantages that make you stand out from the competition. Although this strategy can be profitable, it may turn off clients who are price conscious and draw in new rivals.

It's extremely important to set your product or service apart in competitive markets by emphasizing its special characteristics and advantages.

The more you highlight exclusivity or provide value above what your rivals do, the more you'll stand out and be able to charge more."

Important Considerations

Recognizing Your Rivals

Extensive research is necessary to obtain insights on your competitors. It's critical to understand what you're selling, who your competitors are, whether there are any alternatives, and the dynamics of your sector. Use these inquiries as a tool to learn more about your competitive environment:

1. How many rival businesses are present in my market?
2. In comparison to my firm, are my rivals bigger or smaller?
3. Are my rivals located nearby or do they operate from a distance?

4. Are there any obstacles to entry in my business, such as complicated regulations, expensive or specialist equipment requirements, or special ingredients?
5. Is it difficult for newcomers to break into this market?
6. What kind of goods do my rivals sell, and how much of each?
7. What pricing techniques do my rivals use?

A head-to-head comparison of your product prices with those of your competitors could be helpful. It is important to compare net pricing rather than just list prices.

This kind of information can be obtained by phone queries, mystery shopping, openly accessible data, and other means. Throughout this process, pay attention to how the market views your business and its offerings. Make sure your assessment is truthful and reasonable."

Comprehending Your Outlays

The idea of paying your costs and adding a profit margin is fundamental to good pricing. This requires a deep understanding of the cost structure of your goods. It's not just about the direct cost of manufacturing—you have to include all of the necessary parts.

For example, overhead costs include both variable charges like shipping or stocking fees and fixed components like rent. You need to account for these costs when determining the actual cost of your goods.

Many companies make the mistake of either adding all costs in the calculation and overcharging, or excluding some and pricing their items too low. A useful recommendation is to make a monthly spreadsheet that includes all of the charges, such as:

1. The direct costs of manufacturing your goods, such as labor and marketing and sales charges.
2. All operating expenses necessary to keep the business operating and afloat, including any costs related to borrowing money (debt servicing costs).
3. Your pay as the manager or owner of the company.
4. A justifiable yield on the capital that you and other owners or shareholders have invested.
5. Arrangements for upcoming growth and the replacement of deteriorating fixed assets."

Comprehending Your Clientele

Finding out more about your customers requires doing some kind of market research. According to Willett, there are many different ways this research may be done, ranging from simple email surveys with promotional materials distributed to your current client base to more involved and possibly expensive research projects conducted by outside consulting organizations.

Market research companies are able to analyze your market in great detail, dividing up possible clients according to a variety of factors such as price sensitivity, purchase patterns, and demographics.

If you don't have a large budget for market research, you can take a more straightforward approach by grouping customers into a few different categories. These categories could include people who are concerned about their finances, those who value convenience, and people who value prestige.
Your price strategy can be adjusted once your target segment has been determined.``

Surveying Market Trends

Even if you cannot 100% forecast the future, you can keep an eye on outside variables that may affect the demand for your goods in the future. These variables could include anything from long-term weather trends to prospective legislation changes that might have an impact on the sales of your products in the future. In this context, it's also critical to take your competitors' tactics and activities into account."

Continually Examining Your Prices

A key component of a successful pricing plan is to regularly evaluate your prices and the profitability that underlies them, preferably once a month. Merely assessing the total profitability of your business once a month is insufficient. You need to focus on how profitable each of your products is on its own.

It's critical to comprehend just how each product fits into your monthly sales targets. Never forget that respect is earned via careful observation."

More Techniques for Competitive Pricing

1. Customer Engagement: proactively ask your clients for feedback on your pricing strategy. Get input on a regular basis to show that you are dedicated to fulfilling their expectations.

2. Competitive Analysis: If you can't afford to hire a specialized market research team, think about recruiting college students or using other low-cost ways to keep an eye on your rivals' pricing tactics.

3. Budgetary Planning: Make sure you have a strategic road map for your price decisions by creating a thorough pricing strategy that projects out three to six months into the future.

It is imperative that you continue to be uncompromising in your approach to pricing management. Remember that your pricing strategy can have a big influence on whether your firm succeeds or fails."

Chapter 8

How to Get Things Done After Getting Paid

Write a Business Plan

It's important to state your goals clearly right away. Explain exactly what you hope to accomplish and why. Adding an emotional component or a deeper intention to your goals is often effective. For example, your objective could be to do X (getting help, writing a proposal, editing a movie) and simultaneously feel happy, face a fear, be open-minded, or promote candid dialogue.

Establish a deadline for your objective as well. Objectives must be significant enough to take at least thirty days, but no more than three months, to accomplish. Establish the deadline you want to meet.

Next, classify your objectives while taking internal and external factors into account. If your objective is to create a website, for example, this can include things like working with a graphic designer, writing content for the website, choosing the website's style, organizing a free offer, and more.

Managing any anxiety you may have about contract work could be an internal objective. Divide these objectives into manageable chunks.

Make each goal as attainable as you can by breaking them up into reasonable, one- to two-hour time intervals. If your objective is to create a website, for instance, one step you may do is to look up websites with designs you like.

The idea is to break up the work into manageable chunks so that you don't get overwhelmed or run out of time. Lastly, plan them into your calendar. Once your goals have been broken down into doable steps, incorporate them into your schedule by assigning responsibilities for each week, resulting in a well-organized strategy that you can adhere to."

Comprehending the Business Context of Your Client

It is critical to have a thorough understanding of your client's business. Make a basic profile of your client first. Find out if the customer is a privately held or publicly traded corporation. Whereas private clients could be more difficult to get data from, they frequently have the information available upon request.

Publicly traded clients, on the other hand, usually have a wealth of readily available internet information. Request internal studies, financial accounts, or any other pertinent data the customer thinks might be helpful.

Analyze the magnitude of the client. Several variables, including yearly sales, market capitalization, revenue, yearly profits, total assets, and the number of employees, can be examined in order to accomplish this.

Take into account how intricate the client's business is. Examine elements such as the variety of products or business lines, look into the capital and corporate structure, and ascertain whether the company works in regulated or unregulated industries in order to determine complexity. Find out the client's worldwide reach as well, taking into account the number of nations it works in and the size of its personnel.

It is equally important to comprehend the decision-making process of the client. It's critical for legal counsel to understand decision-making processes and decision-makers. Examine the company culture to see if it is more entrepreneurial or bureaucratic in nature.

Learn about the workings of the Board of Directors and find out if authority is delegated or if senior management must approve every action."

Creating a Weekly Action Plan to Reach Your Objectives

Clear goal-setting becomes essential in demanding work situations. You need a plan to achieve your goals in addition to clear objectives if you want to steer clear of bad situations and succeed instead.

Developing an action plan, which is a comprehensive and workable approach that can be used to any objective you establish, is always the key to successfully achieving your goals. No matter what kind of dream you have, creating a clear and concise action plan is essential to turning it from a vague notion into a concrete reality.

In actuality, business professionals have a much higher likelihood of success when they set measurable targets. This is defining the resources, time, and financial commitments needed to reach your goals in addition to just stating what they are.

Reaching your objectives, no matter how big or small, doesn't require extraordinary intelligence or skill. It requires unshakeable resolve, perseverance, and most importantly, a workable action plan. It's like planning to fail and not planning at all.

Start by writing down your objectives. After that, start figuring out how to get from where you are now (Point A) to where you want to end up (Point Z). Writing down your thoughts, on paper or in digital form, forces you to think analytically and may lead to new discoveries.

This is how your action plan begins. Next, divide your goal into smaller, more doable tasks, each with a reasonable completion date.

Decide on your metrics for measuring your development; they act as a reality check. Finally, specify the amount of money, time, energy, and research that must be invested in each phase. Evaluate the resources at your disposal and determine what more is required to carry out your plan successfully."

Tracking and Evaluating Development"

Maintaining a close eye on your company's performance is essential to maximizing output and profit. To make the most impact, whether you are a lone proprietor or oversee a group of workers, you must use your time and talents effectively.

Many things affect productivity, such as putting in place efficient processes, setting priorities for your work, and keeping yourself and your team motivated.

Any successful commercial activity is built on a well-defined plan. However, it's crucial to set up time to carefully examine each of your processes before coming up with methods. This means analyzing the projects you work on, the motivations behind them, the results they produce, and the way you approach them.

Developing a plan of action only becomes possible once this evaluation is finished. Setting and achieving specific goals is essential to knowing where you're going. It's critical to steer clear of the typical error of making only short-term plans. Thorough understanding of long-term objectives is essential for process optimization and long-term business viability.

Having a clear plan is similar to having goals for both your company and yourself. These goals must be measurable and include measures for both personal and company progress. They can include reaching sales goals and growing your network of business contacts. Reaching these goals can be a great source of inspiration for your team as well as for yourself."

www.ingramcontent.com/pod-product-compliance
Lightning Source LLC
Chambersburg PA
CBHW072053230526
45479CB00010B/929